A SHORT GUIDE TO
Sharing Your Faith

JONATHAN SROCK

Books by Jonathan Srock

A Short Guide to Sharing Your Faith

God's Daily Bread for Your Life: A Devotion for Every Day

Holiness Matters: A Call to Obey the Holy Spirit

Healed in the Name of Jesus: Keep Your Faith in God's Healing Promises

The Passion Chronicles: The Last Week of Jesus' Life

The Greatest Gift Series: 12 Lives Changed by Jesus' Birth

What People Are Saying

"A Short Guide to Sharing Your Faith" by Jonathan Srock is a book for Christian believers who seek guidance in fulfilling their duty to share their faith in Jesus Christ with non-believers. It challenges the Christian believer to take action, equips him with a step-by-step approach to overcome misgivings and feelings of inadequacy, and to share his faith in Jesus. In the end, the reader will come away with a useful and personal approach to this essential mission.

Cathy Ryan, Author
www.cathyryanwrites.com

"In his book, Srock examines the facets of sharing the faith. His intellectual approach will leave the reader equipped in the face of any potential response to the presentation of the Gospel. The brevity of the book will allow for regular review and evaluation of one's own witnessing experiences."

Matthew Niebauer

"I really enjoyed reading A Short Guide To Sharing Your Faith. It contains a great deal of very meaningful information. The parts of the book that clearly spoke to me was hurdles to sharing your faith. Hurdles are very real and the ways to overcome them were helpful. Creating your own approach and sharing your own story verses a canned high pressure approach is very important. The portion on apologetics is very informative. That information is typically not included in evangelism books. Thank you Jonathan is encouraging short story."

Pastor Joe Hollen
Hollentown Assembly of God, Hollentown, PA

"Sharing the good news of Jesus Christ is at the heart of the call on every believer's life. Jon Srock has written a fantastic tool to help guide the newest Christians and the most seasoned saint in sharing the hope that they have in Jesus. This is an easy read with very practical steps to sharing your faith as well as straight-forward advice on how to give answers to the genuine questions people have. I highly recommend both this book and the ministry of Jon Srock. This will encourage, equip and inspire you!"

Pastor Marvin Nemitz
Harvest Community at Church, Jupiter, FL

"I highly recommend Rev. Jonathan Srock's short guide to sharing your faith. This practical resource gives you the tools needed along with the confidence to be able to articulate your faith to others without fear. The 18 common questions that seekers ask and Jonathan's response to those enables the reader to be thoroughly equipped in sharing their faith."

Pastor Zac McDonald
State College Access Church, State College, PA

If you enjoy this book, please subscribe to my website.

Signing up gives you a free gift

and updates to my writings and ministry activity.

Go to www.Jonathansrock.com

Thank you for your support!

A Short Guide to Sharing Your Faith

Jonathan Srock

A SHORT GUIDE TO SHARING YOUR FAITH

Copyright © 2019 Jonathan Srock. All rights reserved. Except for brief quotations in critical publications or reviews, no part of this book may be reproduced in any manner without prior written permission from the publisher. Write: Permissions. Jonathan Srock, 87 Safe Harbor Ln., Smithmill, PA 16680

Jonathan Srock
87 Safe Harbor Ln.
Smithmill, PA 16680

https://www.JonathanSrock.com

ISBN 13: 978-1081739423

Cataloguing-in-Publication Data

A Short Guide to Sharing Your Faith by Jonathan Srock

vi +55 p. ; 23 cm. Includes bibliographical references.
ISBN 13: 978-1081739423
I. Srock, Jonathan
III. A Short Guide to Sharing Your Faith.

CALL NUMBER 2019

Manufactured in the U.S.A.   2019

All Scripture quotations are the translation of the author.

Cover Design: Jonathan Srock with stock photo from

||A Short Guide to Sharing Your Faith

Table of Contents

Acknowledgments i

Introduction iii

Chapter 1 Hurdles to Sharing Your Faith 1

Chapter 2 Confidence to Witness 10

Chapter 3 Types of Evangelism 13

Chapter 4 The Christian Community 17

Chapter 5 Steps to Sharing Your Faith 21

Chapter 6 Apologetics 29

Chapter 7 Leading Seekers to Christ 47

Chapter 8 What's Next? 49

Appendix Resources for Further Engagement 51

Dear Reader 53

About the Author 55

A Short Guide to Sharing Your Faith

Acknowledgments

This guide is an expansion of the Sharing Your Faith series on my blog. I'd like to thank everyone who read and contributed through comments to the discussions there.

I also asked people for questions they face when they share their faith on Facebook and Twitter. Those who have given me suggestions are Leanne Scott. Glenda Lopez Rodriguez, Adam Trimbur, Valda Dracopoulos, and Colleen McCauley.

Several of my beta readers offered book blurbs as well. I'd like to thank Cathy Ryan (www.cathyryan.com), my fellow writer, Matthew Niebauer, one of my closest friends, Pastors Joe Hollen, Marvin Nemitz, and Zac McDonald.

And thank you for picking up this book and reading it. I hope it helps you in your journey to confidence as you share your faith with those around you.

Introduction

If you feel unprepared to share your faith with others, this book is for you. The hurdles facing Christians paralyze them and keep them from sharing their faith. But anyone can overcome any issue holding them back. The world needs to hear your story and your experience with Jesus.

I designed this short guide to help you grow in the concepts of personal evangelism and provide a practical help in sharing your faith. Its aim is to explain the why's and how's of evangelism. I want to encourage you to get out there and share your faith with confidence.

There are many resources for evangelism. This guide exposes common issues I noticed throughout my pastoral ministry and personal life. I've run into many of the same issues presented in this book.

Our Mandate

No matter what your personality, Jesus calls you to share with everyone you know about him. There is no escaping such a calling. Some Christians have this gift, but Jesus expects everyone to evangelize.

Some Christians are more "successful" than others. But we use human and worldly methods to define success. The most common metric for success in evangelism is the amount of people a person "brings to Christ." Do our efforts leading up to the salvation prayer mean nothing?

Some are not confident enough to even try to share their faith. But others give up for various reasons, including, "I'm the quiet one. Someone else has more skill and experience than me." Maybe you tried it once, thought you failed, and gave up. Being judged by improper standards on your evangelistic efforts is cruel and depressing.

Jesus did not require us to save people. He did not command us to "enforce" the gospel. We shouldn't be nervous, fearful, or dejected when we share Jesus with our world. But he didn't leave us with an excuse when we don't do it either.

The Great Commission

Christians I encounter know the Great Commission forward and backward. Every missionary, pastor, and Christian speaker pleads from the pulpit for us to share Jesus. They reference Matthew 28:19-20 regularly. But this passage can be tricky.

Proper understanding of the Great Commission ensures greater success in witnessing. Bible translations don't help the matter much. Highlighting the main actions makes Matthew 28:19-20 clearer. Most versions make "going" the main verb. It is better translated:

"Therefore, after going, make disciples of all nations, continuously baptizing them in the name of the Father, and the Son, and the Holy Spirit, continuously teaching them to observe everything I commanded you–and behold, I keep being with you all the days until the completion of the age" (Matthew 28:19-20, author's translation).

This shows what Jesus emphasized in the passage. "Make disciples" is the main action. Now, everything else helps us to accomplish that goal. "After going" demonstrates the need to make disciples in our everyday travels. No matter where you are, you are standing in the middle of the mission field. And you are the missionary.

No matter who we meet, we are to make disciples, people who want to learn from, commit themselves to, and follow Christ. I translated baptizing and teaching in the continuous present, a technical way of saying that we never stop doing these things. This means we must keep making disciples so we can keep baptizing and teaching them. You never stop learning about Jesus.

It's also important to remember that God's presence is with us always. He is with us every time we open our mouths to talk about him. He has also promised that the Holy Spirit will give us the words to speak (Luke 12:12). There is not one day Jesus takes a break until the end of time. We should encourage one another to reach out and speak up for him. He's got our backs!

The Great Commitment

It's easy to claim misunderstanding of the Great Commission or to say someone else is more effective than you at witnessing. But you won't experience greater ability or success by hiding behind excuses. It's time to get out there and commit to obeying Scripture and the God who spoke it.

After hearing God's Word on the matter and going through this short guide, there is virtually nothing to hide behind anymore. It is time to act. It is my goal to encourage you, but to not allow you to hide behind excuses any longer. Jesus expects each of us to share our faith as his followers.

Dare I say that if you are not witnessing to others, at the very least trying, you may not be a practicing Christian. Those are harsh words, but until each of us places a premium on Jesus' command, we will remain ineffective and unchanged.

The only way to become a more effective witness and representative of Christ is to start with a commitment to go above and beyond Jesus' call of duty. Even if you don't think you're able to discuss the finer points of God's principles in the Bible, he tells us what to do in black and white. The only recourse left is to act.

I encourage and challenge you to step out of your comfort zone and make a commitment to Jesus that you will do what he commanded in his Word. Take advantage of every resource to become the best witness you can be. Share what Jesus has done in your life with everyone around you. Before you learn any principles or pointers on how to share your faith better, the commitment must be your top priority.

Our Mission

There is an entire world in the dark out there. As many Christian missionaries I have heard say, "If someone is thirsty, and you have a cup of cold water, how could you withhold it from them?" We have the words of life and we know the Light of the World. How could any of us keep others from this life-giving Lord?

We have our mission. Think back to the moment of your own salvation and how Jesus changed your life in an instant. Could any of us keep anyone from him? Philip could not stop himself from telling Nathaniel about Jesus (John 1:45) and we should have that same passion.

The only way to fulfill your mission given to you by Jesus is to have the passion to share. Let nothing hold you back, not fear, feeling inadequate, or anything else. No one else can stand before God for you. Each one of us is responsible for our own commitment and response to his call. Step out and embrace the mission with your whole being!

Chapter 1
Hurdles to Sharing Your Faith

Fear of Rejection

The most widely used argument I have heard in my ministry is that people are afraid of being rejected by family, friends, and strangers. Some try to combat this by telling Christians, "They're not rejecting you; they're rejecting Jesus." The problem is that you represent Jesus and they are rejecting you because you serve him.

The pain of rejection stings deeply. Nobody enjoys being rejected. Those rejected in society are usually planning, or dreaming of, vengeance against their adversaries. Because no one seeks rejection, what could motivate us to share Jesus?

- Is your friend/family member's eternal destiny more important than your comfort?
- If you had the cure for a terminal illness, wouldn't you want to give it?
- Is beating around the bush bringing them closer to Jesus?
- How much time do you think they have before it's too late?
- If they would defriend you for talking about Jesus for two to three minutes, were they really your friends?

These are hard questions and thoughts. But if we are not honest with our fear of rejection, it will master us. They will never hear about Jesus. We must step out of our comfort zone and deliver the message Jesus gave us. Their eternal life depends on it.

How do we get rid of the fear of rejection? The first step is to put it in its place. Fear is the devil talking. Every time you let rejection keep you from sharing, he wins. One moment of rejection, or even humiliation (dare we call it persecution?) is worth the 59possibility of your family member/friend/loved one/stranger coming to Jesus.

Until you and I are okay with humiliation, embarrassment, and persecution for Jesus' sake, we will not be doing what he called us to do. It would be nice if people reacted in a calm, civil way. But even Jesus warned us of persecution for his sake (Matthew 5:10-11; 24:9 Luke 21:12, 17; Acts 9:16). The Bible tells us that the cross is an offense (1 Corinthians 1:18; Galatians 5:11). Rejection is built-in to the message of the Gospel.

Second, swallow your pride and serve Jesus. Put the thought of rejection out of your mind. Physically step forward and listen to the Holy Spirit. He is going before you to prepare the way. Trust that he will give you the words to speak.

Look for a place in the conversation to link it to Jesus. This isn't easy at first, but the more you do it, the more you will feel the leading of the Holy Spirit. God will surprise you with the doors he opens for you. But it all begins with sharing your faith by speaking to others.

To be sure, eternity is a heavy matter. But until we get uncomfortable with people dying without Jesus forever, we're not doing our job. Any Christian not sharing Jesus with people who don't know him have a questionable faith.

Action Steps for Fear of Rejection

- Put fear in its place.

- Realize the Gospel is an offense for rejection.

- Trust the Holy Spirit to lead you.

- Physically step toward the person and prepare for your opportunity.

- &Connect Jesus to the conversation and tell your story.

Tongue-Tied and Speechless

For some Christians, fear of rejection is not nearly as bad as having a conversation with someone. For whatever reason, they are afraid to speak out. Perhaps they have several of these fears. But don't let fear rule you or become an excuse.

The person you want to share your faith with may be more afraid to address their issues or questions. They may never walk up to you and ask about your faith. That's why it's up to you to start the conversation with them.

So you're shy, but it's not the end of the world. Conversations with strangers may not be in your wheelhouse, but don't start there. Start with a friend or family member, someone you know. Pick someone you are comfortable with.

It's up to you. Jesus commissioned you and trusts you with this person's soul. He put you in their world and you may be the only Christian they know. If he trusts you, take that as confidence and reach out.

- Sometimes, you just need a little motivation. Think about this:

- If you don't tell them, no one will.

- Their eternal salvation is more important than your comfort.

- You want them to be in heaven with you and Jesus.

- No matter what happens, Jesus is with you (Matthew 28:20).

- The Holy Spirit will give you the words to speak (Mark 13:11; Acts 4:8; 6:10; 13:9).

I know it's a daunting task, but you can do it. The Holy Spirit has gone before you to prepare the person to hear what you have to say. Don't be afraid. We'll be discussing some pointers on how to start the conversation and get the ball rolling. But the best thing you can do is step out in faith and do your best.

Starting the Conversation

Many people do well with conversation starters, icebreakers, and other models to get them started. If they had these kinds of resources, they would feel much more confident. So here are some ways to get the ball rolling.

No matter what situation you find yourself in, there is always a way to start the conversation about your faith. If the person you're sharing with doesn't bring it up, you can do it. But first, we must address a few important points.

Look for ways to begin the conversation. If you know the person and their situation, you can offer them God's help. This is often a great way to get a person involved in the conversation about Jesus. There's often an initial need people have that makes them think about God and becoming a Christian.

If this is not the case, and the person thinks they are doing just fine, one of the best ways to enter the conversation about

Jesus is to ask them what they think of him. No matter who I've talked to, they always have an opinion about Jesus Christ. It could be negative, or it could be positive. Ask them what they think of him.

Another avenue to explore with them is whether they think they're going to heaven or not. Usually this enters the question of their morality. Most people compare themselves to bad people so they feel they are good enough to enter heaven. You can bring up the fact that good works don't get us into heaven. Only a relationship with Jesus will.

Finally, you need to prepare for the encounter and conversation you will have with them. Here are a few steps you should take before you even broach the conversation event:

- **Pray for the person you will witness to.** Whether God has placed a family member, friend, coworker, colleague, or even a complete stranger on our hearts, we must begin before we open our mouths with bowing our knees. We need to get a heart to see that person come to Jesus. We need to observe their need for him. We need to have a passion to see them know Jesus before we speak.

- **Ask God to prepare their heart.** God goes before us and prepares others to hear what we have to say. We are not alone. We are following in his footsteps. He tills the soil, making hard ground soft to hear the gospel. We are partnering with God in asking him to prepare them. We move from the passive role of saying, "That guy needs Jesus" to "Lord, make him aware of his need for you and send me!"

- **Ask God for boldness and openness to the Spirit.** Even though God gives us the words to speak, we must be open and sensitive to the Holy Spirit to hear them. Often when I have spoken to others about Jesus, I am surprised to hear what comes out of my mouth. It is almost as if the Holy Spirit is using me and I am taking a backseat. This is how it should be. We cannot be like Jonah and run the opposite way when God tells us to speak. The Spirit will give you the boldness to speak his words he has for that person.

After you have prepared for the conversation, step out in faith and begin it. The worst thing that will happen is that they will reject you or they will ask you something you don't know the answer to. We will cover that further in this guide.

Fear of Answering Questions

Some people are afraid to share their faith because of the biggest monster, questions. They put you on the spot. The person you're witnessing to could ask anything. Would they ask a question you don't know the answer to?

There's a strategy for dealing with questions from seekers. But there are different kinds of questions they can ask you. They usually fall into these categories:

- **Personal questions.** These deal with your personal story or why you are a Christian. The person can ask you anything about your life or your opinion on God, the Bible, etc. These are the easiest questions because there is nothing involved except your personal answer. If you don't have one for the subject, you can develop it.

- **Faith questions.** Most people who don't believe in Jesus have a reason. It usually has something to do with Christianity itself. They might hold back because they think Christians are hypocrites or they have a problem with what they would think is a strange belief. They could ask about different denominations. Usually they have a misunderstanding of one of these. This may require some research, but you can give your opinion on the matter. If you have to research, you can ask them to return to the issue in a later conversation, research it, and then address it again.

- **Philosophical questions.** The hardest questions to answer are those that have to deal with the expanse after religion into philosophy. They may mean to trap you with their questions. Others are questions about things you may or may not have heard of within Christianity. They will require research. Your best option is to tell them you are unsure but will find out the answer to the best of your ability. I've found one of the best ways to address these issues is to explain that sometimes faith is stepping into the unknown. Tell them you need time to consider their question. It shows that you care.

When you encounter a question you don't know how to answer, ask the person for time to research for them. If they are seriously seeking to learn about God, especially an agnostic (a person genuinely seeking the truth) they will appreciate your attention to detail. If they don't understand that no one has all the answers on their own, they will respect the fact that you are researching the answer for them.

Finally, some people ask questions to trip you up or distract you. But this doesn't mean your best efforts are in vain. Most people who are considering your faith will give you time to find the answers they are looking for. When you take their questions seriously, you gain respect. If you don't know the answer after consulting every resource you have (your pastor, books, etc.), be honest and tell them you don't know the answer.

Important: Don't snow your person over and act like you know everything. That's a big turnoff for seekers. Honesty and genuine care for their questions avoid making you look fake to them.

Someone Else Will Do It

There are uncommitted Christians who trust in evangelists and their pastor to lead people to the Lord. But Jesus gave us the Great Commission because he wants to involve each of us in spreading his good news of his kingdom.

There's no room to be lazy. The time is short until Jesus returns. We must do our best to use our influence in our world. There are people you know that no other Christian can reach. You don't even realize the influence you have in people's lives around you.

God placed you in your situation in life, your personal mission field, to reach the people he has placed around you. He planted you like a flower in choice soil. God expects you to grow, for your roots to reach everyone you meet. Reach out and share the life-giving good news you have. Don't keep it to yourself.

Consider yourself the last ditch effort, God's extended hands to that person. You are their last line of defense against eternal condemnation. If you don't share your faith, they will never hear of relationship with Jesus and the benefits of salvation. It's up to you and you can do it!

Having to Do It All

One of my biggest fears when I first began sharing my faith was that I would have to lead someone from atheism to Christianity. Walking a person through the steps of seeking faith can be a long journey. And some people never reach the destination.

I always felt it would be my fault if they did not get there. But I began to learn an invaluable lesson. I'm not a one-man band. I don't have to do it all. I am a cog in the wheel of the Holy Spirit's work in that person's life.

He may only use me once to nudge that person closer to Jesus. You may play a greater role in a seeker's journey. But you're not the one at fault or to blame if they don't make it to the destination of knowing Jesus.

You're not the one who saves a person. That is the work of the Holy Spirit. The only thing you could feel ashamed about is if you do not obey the Holy Spirit when he tells you to help bring them closer to Jesus. Don't be afraid to play your part or parts.

The Holy Spirit uses us as his instruments for whatever he sees fit. When he uses you, he trusts you with that part of the process. He has trained you for that task. He knows the tools in his toolbox. It's an honor when he calls on you to help in a seeker's journey to salvation.

Chapter 2
Confidence to Witness

I've met many Christians over the years who have hang-ups about witnessing. It doesn't help when you see someone on the street with a "Turn or Burn" sign. There are many ways to share your faith, and I want this guide to encourage you and give you the confidence you need to witness to others.

The Bible calls us to share our faith (Matthew 28:19). But some people are uncomfortable sharing their faith. There are many programs out there, but some of them have a rigid design that doesn't take into account our personalities and the way we communicate with others.

Some people are bold and have no trouble with high-pressure situations. Their witnessing style can be confrontational without them being uncomfortable. But others are more laid-back, or are better at logical arguments. Still others excel in sharing their story and showing with their life how Jesus has made them different.

These styles and approaches are useful for the right person in the right situation. Our confidence grows with every experience we have in sharing our faith. We learn from every encounter. You will learn what works best for you. But knowing what is available will help you start out without having to use trial and error from the very beginning.

God has placed each of us in a different environment no one else has the ability and influence to share Jesus. We know sharing our faith is our mission as Christians, but having the advantage of knowing your style and your abilities gives you confidence.

A Short Guide to Sharing Your Faith

In your community, your family, your workplace, your school, and any other context God places you, you can be the best at sharing your faith in your way. I designed this guide to spur you on to great success in sharing your faith with others.

Everyone struggles with some part of sharing their faith. Whether it's the mechanics where the information we need to know to share our faith, or even the confidence to step out and begin talking, you are not alone. No one is perfect, and Jesus didn't call us to perfection in sharing our faith.

He only calls us to step out and follow the leading of the Holy Spirit. He calls us to have compassion on those around us who don't know him. We are soldiers in a spiritual battle with limited time to act. These battles can easily raise our anxiety levels.

We want to be successful for Jesus' sake, and for the sake of those we love so they will join us in heaven for eternity. The stakes are high, but we can please Jesus with our efforts. The best part is that no one is so far gone from grace that God cannot reach them.

It's time to step up and step out in faith. Lay all of your fears aside. God chose you to talk to that person. God laid that person on your heart. He will go before you and go with you. I hope that this guide will help you gain the confidence to share your faith with confidence and comfort.

Chapter 3
Types of Evangelism

High Pressure Approaches

These approaches involve confrontational approaches like street evangelism and door-to-door evangelism. It also includes programs that ask the listener questions.

One approach is the Ten Commandments approach. Ask the person if they believe they will go to heaven. Often people play the karma card where their good deeds outweigh their bad. But it springs the trap.

Taking one commandment at a time, ask them if they've ever broken it. Invariably, they will admit that they have. Once they do, explain that it's not about what you do but who you know that gets you to heaven. That is the springboard into the conversation.

Another is the very famous Evangelism Explosion that uses similar tactics. When it first came out, trained teachers taught it to their students. I'm unsure if it's still that way today.

Such programs help people to share their faith. They give you a template for sharing your faith that is empowering at first, but these programs rely on memorization and you to start the conversation. Not all approaches to evangelism have these requirements.

Confrontational Evangelism

We're all familiar with the guys on street corners yelling through bullhorns or holding up signs that say, "Turn or Burn." Maybe you've run into someone who seemed to yell the gospel at you.

Nobody wants to be on the receiving end of the in-your-face experience. But some people seem to have the personality for being the ones to confront others. All the drama that comes with confrontation rarely helps anyone.

If you've got that special gift of confrontation that seems to be effective, that's great. But from my experience most people don't do confrontation well on either end.

The gospel has a confrontational side to it. The Bible speaks of the cross being a stumbling block (1 Corinthians 1:22-24). The problem is that people don't always catch the spirit of kindness in confrontational approaches.

People often use slogans on signs, bumper stickers, and T-shirts. But slogans minimize knowledge on any topic. It's impossible to include all the views and information in a slogan. "Turn or burn" is not an accurate picture of salvation and condemnation. Ask yourself, "Would Jesus carry that sign?"

Our approach to witnessing must show what Christianity is all about. Yelling does not come off in our culture as anything other than anger. Jesus didn't ostracize the sinners in his culture; he took the religious leaders to task.

Each of us must witness that is effective, accurate to Jesus' teachings, and comfortable for us to use. Only then will we have the confidence to show Christianity to the world.

Door-to-Door and Street Evangelism

Door-to-door evangelism is closely related to street evangelism. They both use the same methods. These both fall under high pressure approaches to sharing your faith. They work for some people, especially outgoing people.

Door-to-door evangelism happens when you walk up to a stranger's door, knock, and use one of these memorization programs to speak with whoever answers the door. You continue to canvas throughout the whole neighborhood or area.

A Short Guide to Sharing Your Faith

The problems with this approach are that you invade that person's home. This approach resembles approaches by others, such as Mormons and Jehovah's Witnesses, that are not popular. The level of rejection may be higher with this approach than with others.

Street evangelism uses the same tactics as door-to-door evangelism, except that most of the action happens on the street. You walk up to a person and begin a similar conversation as you would at someone's door.

This has the same drawbacks as door-to-door evangelism. From time to time they show some effectiveness, but they have a high rate of rejection and bitterness from those who experience them.

Lifestyle Evangelism

Unlike the high pressure approaches discussed above, lifestyle evangelism focuses on witnessing through action. If you are following biblical principles in your life and obeying Jesus' teachings and the Holy Spirit, your life will look different from the world's.

It will be very noticeable to everyone around you. Especially when you follow Jesus yourself, those closest to you will notice the big changes. Often, your loved one's need to hear about Jesus.

Your lifestyle with Jesus in control is like a billboard advertisement to the world. They are watching everything you do now that you have proclaimed you are a Christian. Because they are watching you, noticing how different you are, some will become curious.

Through the choices you make and the actions you take, you open the door to sharing your faith with others. As they become interested in the positive differences in your life, it provides a way for you to start a conversation with your lifestyle. You don't even have to say a word.

Lifestyle evangelism is a powerful tool to get your foot in the door on sharing your faith, but it is not enough on its own. You still must open your mouth and tell people about Jesus. But interest in your changed lifestyle is a good start on sharing your faith.

Compassion Ministry

Sometimes the best way to start the conversation about your faith is to help others in need. Often people follow Jesus because of a trial or rough situation in their lives.

They need someone to help them, a Savior. If there are people going through rough times in their life, they may be more open to hearing about Jesus. Helping them with a need they have will make sharing your faith all the easier.

When they realize that you noticed their plight and make the effort to help them with it, you've opened their heart when you tell them it's because of Jesus that you are providing for their need. When Jesus gets the credit, their hearts are open to receive the message of the good news of your faith.

Once again, providing for someone's needs without telling them why you're doing it is not sharing your faith. They must know exactly why you would notice them and help them. People never expect to receive help from others. The world doesn't work that way.

But you must open your mouth and speak about Jesus. Once they hear about your motivation for helping them, they are usually interested to find out more. This is your open door to share your faith with them.

Chapter 4
The Christian Community

Encouraging One Another

Jesus instituted the church for several reasons, but one benefit of the community of faith is to help one another. Christians are in a world that rejects their Savior and them. We would be on our own if it weren't for the body of Christ.

One of the best things we can do for one another is encouraging each other. We all have different trials and struggles in life. But basking in God's presence with his people invigorates us to continue serving him with excellence.

When we have troubles, we can lean on one another. The church is in place so we take care of one another (Acts 2:42-47). The world is our desert, but the church is our oasis.

This is how it's supposed to be. It is and always has been this way for every believer. Sometimes we don't connect to the church as we should, and other times we don't find another believer that will help us. But this isn't how it should be.

If you can't count on your spiritual family, who can you count on? Jesus instituted the church on earth for this. So we find ways of encouraging one another, lifting one another's spirits.

We teach each other how to be successful in serving Jesus, including sharing our faith with others. Those who have experience in this area, such as evangelists or those with the evangelistic gift, can teach others how to share as they do.

We are stronger together because we serve Jesus by serving each other. When one Christian feels like he or she is failing at witnessing, turning to another Christian who excels in evangelism and can teach them will boost our confidence.

Other times people simply need to hear that they're doing a good job. We need to encourage them and tell them they can do it. They may not see in themselves what other Christians see, the positive and life-giving force of sharing their story with others in the world.

Let's be team players. When another Christian does well at witnessing and sees success, we need to celebrate with them. When someone is struggling with sharing their faith, we need to come alongside of them, teach them, and encourage them. The whole kingdom of Jesus is served when we help one another.

Equipping One Another

Sharing your faith is not only personal but also enhanced with equipment. Christians need to come alongside one another and give them the tools to succeed at sharing their faith.

Equipping each other to share our faith requires us to share our experiences and what we've learned. Teaching others is a way for all of us to get better at the skill of witnessing.

Your personal style, story, and experiences will color your approach to witnessing. But there is always something new to learn from others. Everything from practicing sharing your faith with other believers to hearing their approach can be helpful.

To get the most out of equipping others, we need to adopt certain characteristics. First, we must be teachable and humble. No one knows everything about the best practices for sharing our faith. We can all learn from one another.

Second, experiences gained through practice of the lessons we learn. It may sound strange to practice sharing your faith with another believer. It might even seem canned or fake. But working through the mechanics of witnessing gives you practice and makes you better.

Finally, being genuine when you share your faith might be the most important of these characteristics. People can smell hypocrites and fake people from a mile away. They will reject a person trying to put a notch in their spiritual belt or gain spiritual points. It's not about you when you share your faith. It's about what Jesus has done for you and what he can do for the person you witness to.

Everyone needs a little help along the way. We can all learn something that will help us excel at witnessing. Do everything you can and gain every piece of knowledge and wisdom about sharing your faith.

Be the best that you can be. If you can enhance your witnessing ability, it helps the seeker to understand Jesus more clearly. It's worth all of your efforts!

Empowered to Witness

We talked about having the confidence to share your faith earlier. Some principles and lessons you learn as you share your faith and connect with the community of faith will set your ability to witness on fire.

You'll see better results and more people beginning to follow Jesus. Most of all, partnering with the Holy Spirit in witnessing will empower you with confidence rather than pride.

The ultimate task of achieving our mandate for Jesus and fulfilling the Great Commission energizes us and boosts our confidence. We want to keep sharing. Between the church and the spirit, we receive everything we need to be effective in serving Jesus and the unsaved.

Instead of hiding behind hurdles or worrying about success in sharing our faith, we get excited about the results. Focus on the possibility that your unsaved loved ones, friends, coworkers, colleagues, and everyone around you will join you for eternity.

The Holy Spirit and Witnessing

For some people, it is a controversial issue. But as a Pentecostal, I believe one key to boldly sharing your faith is baptism in the Holy Spirit. In Acts 2:1-4, the Holy Spirit came upon the disciples like never before.

He rested on them in tongues of fire, fulfilling Jesus' ability to baptize with fire (Luke 3:16). The Holy Spirit empowered them to witness with a boldness they didn't have before. Not only were they unafraid to share their faith, but they shared it in a fresh way.

In Acts 2:11, we see the result of this empowerment. They shared their faith with people who speak a different language. The Spirit broke down the language barrier, and they proclaimed God's glory in the original language of everyone around them from 13 places (Acts 2:7-11).

While we may not always speak other languages for the people we share our faith with, that same boldness and empowerment to not be afraid and to follow the Holy Spirit's lead is available to every Spirit-filled believer. All you have to do is ask him to guide you, give you the words to speak, and step out in faith.

We must rely on the Holy Spirit in every aspect of sharing our faith. He makes us bold and able to share. He comes alongside of us and leads us to share and glorify Jesus.

Chapter 5
Steps to Sharing Your Faith

Prayer

It's often skipped by many Christians, but it's the most important step in anything we do. How can we expect God to bless our efforts in sharing our faith if we don't ask him to guide us first? We will be much more effective if he leads us to the right people at the right time and gives us the right words to speak.

What should the content of such prayers be? What should we focus on when we pray about sharing our faith?

- **Pray for the right person.** Doesn't God want everyone to be saved? Yes. But there's a process with each person. Some people are more ready than others, and only God knows people's hearts. Ask God to send you to the right person.
- **Pray for the right time.** Many Christians worry about when to speak to others. The best time to share about Jesus is when the Holy Spirit tells you to. This requires listening to the Holy Spirit throughout our day. He will prompt us to share when the time is right.
- **Pray for the right place.** Should I share in public or in private? Should I witness at work, invite them for coffee, call them at home, or at some other place? This may depend on the person, whether they are comfortable in public or private. Rarely does the environment matter as much as the message.

- **Pray for the right words.** God gives us the words to speak by the Spirit's power. He helps with transitions and introductions in the conversation. They may say, "I feel like I'm alone in this situation," or "I'm curious about God but don't know where to start." Pay attention to these cues and prompts. Be sensitive to the Spirit's leading.

Taking these steps in prayer means that we are being intentional about sharing our faith. Follow the Spirit's leading. Even more, it takes the pressure off of us to come up with the right person, time, place, and words. God is working these things out and going before us.

Remember that God wants to use you. He sees everything he planted in you and uses you for his plan to save those around you. Don't be afraid to share your faith! He handpicked you to speak to that person because he knew he could trust you with their soul.

Divine Appointments

You hear about them all the time in church, those elusive divine appointments. Are they moments with God? Or are they special times of renewal? A divine appointment is when the Holy Spirit leads you to the right person at the right time with the right result.

The Spirit leads us in our daily walk with Jesus, but he does a lot more. Just as we can hear his voice as we read God's Word and pray, he also leads us in sharing our faith.

As part of your prayer process, begin asking the Spirit to lead you to the right person. Then ask him to give you the words to speak. When prompted by him, the event of speaking to the right person at the right time with the right words is the divine appointment.

This is Spirit-empowered witnessing at the next level. When you work in concert with God and his plans for the people you share your faith with, he goes before you and prepares them to receive the message. This makes it so much easier to share your faith. You are operating within God's will!

Divine appointments are not some mystical, spiritual experience. God gives them to people he trusts to speak about Jesus and demonstrate his transformation in them. You receive divine appointments when you ask the Spirit to lead you in sharing your faith. Then, follow his lead and his prompting.

Grace and Truth

John talks about grace and truth when we witness to others (John 1:14). Jesus was full of them and we need to be as well. We will be more effective when we tap into both as we witness.

We must be gracious when we speak about Jesus to others. Treating them with respect and being kind gains more listeners willing to hear what we have to say. If we are arrogant about our faith, they won't want to be a part of it.

Grace yields more results than anger or pride. People can sense these feelings in us. They know when they're being disrespected. We enter their world and they are being gracious enough to listen to us. We must do the same.

But we must not allow grace to overpower the truth. The truth is that people are steeped in sin and need a Savior. The truth is that people who don't know Jesus aren't going to heaven. We need to present these truths with power.

Christians tend to lean to one of these poles. Either they don't want to step on people's toes and are too gracious or they present the truth of the Gospel without kindness or respect. We must find a balance between grace and truth.

When you talk about Jesus, tell people the truth of their situation. But do it out of love. Let them know that you want to see them in heaven with you. Don't say this in a rude way like you are superior to them because you already know Jesus.

Your heart for the person must come through every time you speak. If you are not genuine, this is how they'll know. Jesus never disrespected anyone he spoke to, but he didn't mince words when he told them the truth.

Telling Your Story

I believe the best way to open the conversation about your faith is to tell your story. Everyone loves a good story. The greatest story ever told, other than Jesus' story, is your story of how he changed your life.

Especially in the New Testament, the writers talk about two lives, the old life and the new life with Christ. There's a separation from the way you used to be before you met Jesus and after he transformed you.

You can tell they're addressing it when they say things like, "Formerly, you had a wicked lifestyle, but now God has set you free." I'm paraphrasing how they describe it, but some examples are Ephesians 2:1-4 and Romans 6:6-7.

There are several benefits to opening conversation about Jesus with your personal story:

- **It takes the pressure off.** For anyone who is shy, struggles to talk openly with others, worries about answering hard questions, or is uncomfortable in high-pressure situations, this allows you to share what you know.
- **No one can refute it.** No one can challenge what Jesus has done for you. They can't tell you you're wrong. It tells them about Jesus from a personal standpoint and shows them he still works today.
- **It's not a canned answer.** People may complain that your answers to their questions aren't yours. They claim they've heard that answer before and you got it out of some book. But that claim is void when it's a fresh story.
- **It's unique to you.** Because this is your story, it's unlike anything else they would have already heard. It's a personal

look into what Jesus did for you. It's a fresh statement of Jesus' power to change your life.
- **It's eyewitness testimony.** Historians say the best type of history is first-hand accounts of an event. They solidify that it happened in reality. Telling your story shows first-hand evidence that Jesus is real. No one can say that Christianity isn't helping you.

Your testimony is powerful, even if you don't think so. I always thought my testimony was weak because I grew up in church. I didn't have a groundbreaking, earth-shattering testimony about being saved from drugs, alcohol, or crime. But people are still interested in my story. Any story that tells of Jesus' power to save us from sin, hell, and the grave can be used by the Spirit to lead others to Jesus.

Don't be afraid to share your story. It's as easy as sharing your background and why you're different now. Take time to write it down and master it.

By master it, I don't mean memorize. I mean know your story and highlight how Jesus changed you. Give him all the credit and glory. Every time you share your story, it will be a little different, but that's the Spirit applying it to your listener.

The Invitation

After you tell your story, what should you do next? You summoned your courage to walk up to someone and tell them how Jesus changed your life. That's amazing! But how do you end the conversation?

When I share my story, people ask me questions. Sometimes they're about my story, but other times they are questions burning on their minds about Christianity they never thought they could ask.

But other times they listen and don't push the conversation forward. Here's a simple way to end the conversation with openness to share more later.

Pastors want you to invite people to church. It's about sharing the faith with others, but it can be daunting for visitors. Inviting an interested person to church is a great way to let them know you're available if they need you.

I know that's a crazy proposition because some churches aren't ready for visitors. I realize that. Not every church in America shares a salvation message during their meetings. But if they come, they can meet the pastor and see what it's like.

Here are some suggestions on how to master the invitation and still be genuine:

- **Invite them to a special event.** If the Sunday service won't work for them, try inviting them to a men's group, women's group, life group, or even a special event for those interested in Christianity. They can meet a few Christians without feeling overwhelmed. It also gives them a sense of belonging.
- **Give them a tract or invitation card.** Many invitation cards have the information, so you don't have to explain much. If you use tracts, target the material to the person. If they mentioned they were dealing with something, give them one that might answer some of their questions. Also, as a personal favor, don't give them a tract from 1950.
- **Make it simple and don't apologize.** Many times people apologetically invite others to church. "This is the church I go to. The people are great even if the building is old." Let them decide to attend and form their own opinion about their experience.

If they say yes and attend:

A Short Guide to Sharing Your Faith

- **Welcome them, introduce them, and sit with them.** If you brought someone, you need to be completely involved in making them feel comfortable and welcome. If you don't do it, chances are no one in the church will.
- **Introduce them to the pastor.** Whether it's the pastor preaching or a pastor that would fit their life circumstance (youth pastor for teens, couples pastor for newlyweds, seniors pastor for senior citizens, etc.), you need to show them someone who can connect with them.
- **Take them out to lunch.** Don't let the church be their final experience. Take them out to eat, foot the bill, demonstrate Christian behavior, and ask them if they have questions or comments. This is not about saving their soul. This is about building a friendship with a person who needs Jesus.
- **Make yourself available to them any time they need you.** Sharing your faith is the beginning of a relationship. It's the first step in helping a person know and grow in Jesus. We must be concerned with the whole person rather than one part of them.

Some of these steps may help you as you share your faith. Introducing a person to your faith is an invitation to meet Jesus and other Christians. It's the beginning of a relationship, not the end of our site make yourself available responsibility.

Chapter 6
Apologetics

What Is Apologetics?

Every time I introduce the subject of apologetics, someone asks me, "Why do I have to apologize for my faith?" When you look at the word "apologetics" it looks like "apology." But that's not what the word means.

Apologetics is the systematic study and response of Christians to the questions and observations of unbelievers. It's been around for centuries. Evangelists who shared their faith with the societies around them found people have many questions.

At least a small part of faith is trusting even when you don't understand. But the Bible allows for us to have questions about our faith. These don't have to be questions of doubt. They can be questions to strengthen our belief as well. But it is unbelievers are seeking to understand what they can about Christianity who ask the most questions.

Apologetics comes from a Greek word that Peter uses in his epistle (1 Peter 3:14-16). It means to give an answer back, or to explain. Peter calls all Christians to be prepared to explain or defend their faith. This call is surrounded by some lifestyle evangelism tips.

The way we defend our faith should be done without fear, while honoring Jesus as Lord, with gentleness and respect, and with a good conscience. We shouldn't do it out of anger, and we must remember that Jesus is watching. Apologetics is done to please the Lord and to help others understand the faith.

We must have the right attitude if we will be effective. The goal of apologetics is not to win an argument. It is to see the seeker come to know and serve Jesus. It is to clarify issues of the faith. It should be done in humility and kindness.

Different Types of Apologetics

There are different categories of apologetics. It's more than likely you've at least heard of some of the apologists who focus on these different categories.

- **Logical (Philosophical) Apologetics.** This type of apologetics focuses on reasoning and philosophical debate. They explain misconceptions about the Bible, Christianity, and God. Some examples of logical apologists are William Lane Craig and Norman Geisler.
- **Cultural Apologetics.** This type of apologist focuses on cultural and social issues and how Christianity addresses them. They often seek to show how the Bible's standards deal with today's issues. One example of a cultural apologist is Ravi Zacharias.
- **Scientific Apologetics.** This type of apologetics focuses on the debates between science and religion. They often deal with how science and the Bible mesh or possibly contradict one another. Examples are dealing with creation debates. Frank Turek and Norman Geisler have an excellent book, "I Don't Have Enough Faith To Be An Atheist" that deals with science and faith. Hank Hanegraaff sometimes deals with scientific apologetics. Ken Hamm deals with Creation.

The Need to Learn Apologetics

Some people may ask why they need to defend their faith. It's personal to them and it's none of anyone else's business. But we are called to share it! And when we do, people will have questions.

Think about your own walk with Christ. Do you ever have questions about the Bible, God, or Christianity? There's nothing wrong with questions. In fact, questions are one of the best ways to grow deeper in your faith.

Someone watching from the outside may be interested in Christianity, but afraid to offend us with questions. If you are approached with questions, you must first determine the motive behind them.

Unfortunately, not everyone who asks questions of Christians seeks to learn about God. Some of them have ulterior motives to try to trap us or trip us up. Always look to answer questions from people who are genuinely interested in the faith.

We need to learn how to give a response and defense of our faith because not understanding our own faith can cause doubt in us. Learning more about Christianity, God, and the Bible strengthens and increases our own faith.

Also, how can we tell others what we don't know? If a person asks us a question about Jesus, and we don't know the answer, why would they come to faith in him? This is another way to serve unbelievers who are curious and seeking to know God.

Sometimes answering their questions leads them to a saving faith in Jesus. When they genuinely seek the Lord, and we can help them understand a little bit more about him, it will help them get closer to The Following, knowing, and serving Christ themselves.

How did you come to know and follow Jesus? Chances are it was after you began to understand the faith better. Somebody answered your questions, so it's imperative that you learn how to respond to questions and to defend your faith.

Hurt by the Church

One of the most common reasons I've encountered for people rejecting religion is a deep-seated wound often times placed there by Christians or the church. Whether we meant to hurt them or not, we did.

Sometimes people feel rejected when they visit a church. Other times they have grown up in church but not had their questions answered. Some have found the church offensive to their current beliefs.

It's time to let the healing begin. You may find when you share your faith that people are bitter or angry because they have been hurt when they attempted to learn about Jesus before. They may lash out, trying to hurt you out of their own hurt.

You need to be prepared to face this kind of reaction. They don't do it on purpose. But religion and Christianity may be a sore spot for them because of their pain. One of your goals will be to hear their story, listening with openness and humility.

If at all possible, find out why they are against Christianity and the church. Sometimes you'll find they are not against Jesus or even his teachings, but against the church for the way they were treated in their past.

Whatever their story, sympathize with them. Unfortunately, not every Christian demonstrates Jesus' teachings well all the time. We are all human and make mistakes. Sometimes we don't even realize when we hurt someone else. And they don't always tell us.

Build a relationship of understanding when you discover a wound from the past. Stick with them and show them that not everyone is like the people they have previously known. You may even find that an apology from you will help to begin the healing process.

Even though you didn't commit their hurt, you can show them you are humble enough to take on their story. In the best situation, their heart will be open and tender toward the Lord again.

Hard Atheism

Atheism has been on the rise for several years. It is the belief that God doesn't exist. There is a new wave of atheism called New Atheism. These people are not interested in hearing your questions or a defense of your faith.

They have recently begun campaigns against Christianity and all religion. They see it as dangerous to society. They see it as a crutch for weak people who won't accept their reality.

Some of their most famous representatives are people like Christopher Hitchens, Richard Dawkins, and Sam Harris. They are on the warpath to instill doubt in Christians and eradicate religion of all kinds off the face of the earth.

When they ask questions, they want you to doubt what you believe. They will attack every teaching and doctrine you have ever known. If you give them an inch, they will take a mile.

They make it a personal agenda and life goal to see religion squashed. They will not befriend you and in many cases will not even allow you to get a word in edge wise if they debate you.

You'll be able to tell after sharing your story whether you are dealing with a hard atheist or someone who is open to hearing your message. As harsh as it sounds, if you are dealing with a hard atheist, you are spinning your wheels and will have little to no success. I believe God can reach anyone, but these will be the hardest. Here are some steps you can take with a hard atheist:

1. **Pray that the Holy Spirit will change their heart.** Only the Holy Spirit can know and change a person's heart, preparing them for salvation.
2. **Ask them why they are so against religion and Christianity.** Their answers will tell you more about their background and situation.
3. **Ask them, "What would it take for you to believe in Jesus?"** It may cause them to think about why they have rejected him in the past.

Questions Not Worth Answering?

Hard atheists will raise questions designed to put you on the defensive. If they can get you to doubt your beliefs, they consider it a win. They enjoy challenging everything you say and asking questions that don't have answers.

For instance, two of the most common questions they ask are, "How many angels can fit on the head of a pin?" and, "Can God make a rock so heavy he can't lift it?" The latter question challenges that God is all-powerful.

These kinds of questions are called red herrings in philosophy, questions that are designed to get you off of your message or your answer. They are meant to confuse and cause rabbit trails you may follow.

The attitude with which they are asked clearly portrays the animosity they have toward Christianity. They expect an answer to them as much as you expect them to take you seriously.

These people don't care to learn about God and are not seekers. They will be tough to deal with and you may find yourself completely frustrated. Be cordial and polite, loving and respectful, even though they may not be.

You still represent Jesus. There's always a possibility you may be treated with respect also, and something you say through the Holy Spirit may affect them more deeply than they let on. There's always hope!

Soft Atheism/Agnosticism

Most of your success in sharing your faith will happen with soft atheists and agnostics. An agnostic is someone who is unsure of God's existence. They lean toward his nonexistence, but usually because they feel there is not enough evidence yet.

A soft atheist is a serious seeker who will listen to your message and evidence openly. They are not against you or trying to get you to doubt your faith. They do not have an agenda or a vendetta against you.

These two types tend to be neutral when it comes to religion. Some have really considered religion, grown up without religion, or simply haven't researched it.

Types of Truth

One of the biggest issues you will deal with when you begin to talk to people about your faith is a declaration that it works for you, but doesn't work for them. This is a type of truth that has infected our secular culture.

People have accepted the lie that everything is subjective to every person. Subjective truth does have applications in some categories, but it's usually used to combat absolute truth. People use these different truths to ignore our message.

If you don't understand the difference between these truths, it will be easy to get you off message. To be most effective, you must know these differences. Here are the differences between three truths commonly misunderstood and used in the wrong way:

- **Subjective Truth** – The most commonly held belief that truth only works for certain people in certain situations. "That works for you, but not for me." They are convinced Christianity won't work for them for whatever reason they choose. This is meant to keep you at arm's length. They will state that there are many religions, many ways to God. But they have trouble with discussing which God, and the contradictions within these religions. We live in a postmodern world that questions anything concrete.
- **Absolute Truth** – There are things in this universe that do not change. These are forever statements, descriptions, and rules. No matter what time or environment, you will

always find these things. In a postmodern culture, people have a problem with any of the statements. They may shy away from the idea that Jesus is the only way to get to heaven (John 3:16).

- **Personable Truth** – For Christians, this is the ultimate truth. Pilate asked Jesus, "What is truth?" (John 18:38) But he didn't stick around for the answer. He was a pragmatist who used whatever truth would keep him in power (subjective). Jesus would have answered, "I am the Way, Truth, and Life" (John 14:6). Truth is ultimately represented not in a concept but in the person of Jesus Christ. He is the truth that existed before creation, lives during creation, and will be after creation.

How do you deal with each of these situations when you show your faith? One way you can approach your seeker is to guide them from subjective to personable truth. Since most of the people you will share with begin in subjective truth, the first goal is to give examples of absolute truth that are hard to refute.

Science is a great example for this. Science contains the categories of theories and laws. Theories are ideas of how things work that may or may not be provable. Laws are provable and tested, guaranteed repeated results. Gravity is a law that can easily be proven over and over. Evolution is a theory, not a law. It cannot be proven because no one can repeat the process of evolution or go back and observe it.

Gravity is one of the best absolute truths to point out to people. It does not change. It can be different in different environments, like a lesser gravity on the moon, but it always exists. There's nowhere in the universe that gravity does not play a part in how things work.

Gravity is an absolute truth. Moving from this example, begin speaking of God as the absolute. Bring up passages like John 14:6 where Jesus tells us there is no other way to the Father except through him. Mention the fact that every religion has contrary exceptions to the others. The way to God is different in every religion and God is also different. These differences matter.

You can't follow two religions that contradict one another. Every religion leads you to a different place. Anyone who takes any of these religions seriously must observe these contradictions and exemptions. There's a reason Muslims are against Christian infidels and seek to convert or murder them. It's a fact adopters of subjective truth must deal with.

There are many examples of absolute truth and contradictions in subjective truth. This is where reading and listening to apologetic material will give you ammunition to use in your conversation. Remember to use it with love and kindness.

Once you have them thinking about absolute truth, introduce the question, "Do you believe you're going to heaven when you die?" If they answer yes, ask them, "Why?" Based on their answer, carry on the conversation. If they answer that they don't believe they're going to heaven, continue with the second question.

Most people believe that their works are good enough and that their life is good enough to get into heaven. This is where you transfer them to personable truth. There are two problems with good works:

1. **Everyone has broken God's absolute commandments.** Works won't get us into heaven because we have broken his laws. We are not qualified on our own to go to heaven based on what we've done and how we lived. Using the Ten Commandments or the Romans Road is one approach.
2. **Entrance into heaven is not based on what we do but Who we know.** People who know Jesus go to heaven. If you don't know him, God won't accept you as a citizen of heaven. Personable truth is another approach.

Personable truth is the only way to heaven. The Bible clearly states that Jesus is the only way to the Father in heaven (John 14:6).

Ultimately, since works won't save, the only way to go to heaven is to know Jesus.

Subjective and objective truth fall short in the end. Selectors or It comes down to knowing Jesus personally. When they finally seize this personable truth, the final step is an invitation to accept him as their personal Lord and Savior.

Steps to Discussing Truth

1. Give evidence for absolute truth through examples.
2. Point out that contradictions in religions can't be accepted together. One is right and one is wrong. The question is which one is right.
3. Ask them if they think they're going to heaven and why. Deal with their answer and talk about the only way to get to heaven.
4. Introduce them to Jesus as the Way, Truth, and Life. Depending on how the discussion goes, give them time to consider the conversation, invite them to church, or
5. Lead them in prayer to accept Jesus as their Lord and Savior.

Steps 4 and 5 depend on the way the conversation goes. If your presentation leaves them with food for thought and they want to think about it, don't be pushy. If they are interested enough to want to visit your church or continue the conversation, that's the next step. But if they are ready to accept Jesus, be prepared to take them the rest of the way to the beginning of their life with Jesus.

The Common Questions

Over many years of sharing our faith, Christians have heard questions along the same lines. These questions may be worded differently but are very similar in subject matter and information the seeker is looking for.

A Short Guide to Sharing Your Faith

Apologists throughout the centuries have addressed these questions and can provide answers that please the seeker making it easier for us to share our faith. The first set of questions were asked in a survey I took from my blog series. The second set of questions are from Kenneth Boa.[1] Without further ado, these are some of the most common questions you may be asked. It's not a complete list, but it's a start.

NOTE: Any of the questions in this list or those brought up by the seeker are just a springboard. Your conversation will continue from the question and answer you give. These questions and answers give you credibility and open the door wider for the seeker to dig further. Don't be afraid of the questions that may not be on this list. With further experience you will be able to naturally share your faith. Don't shy away from questions or the conversation that follows.

Questions from My Social Media Survey

1. **Why are there so many different forms of Christianity (denominations)?**

Christianity has several different sects, or denominations. Over the millennia there have been a number of splits usually based on minor doctrinal differences. The main three categories of Christians include Roman Catholics, Orthodox Christians, and Protestants. But all Christians agree on major Christian doctrine. Jesus Christ is Lord and Savior.

2. **How ,you trust a book that has been corrupted?**

There's an assumption that a book lasting as long as the Bible would be corrupt. But this is not the case. Although we no longer have the original manuscripts, the text we have is 99.7% accurate to the original. With the thousands of manuscript pieces collected, we

---

[1] Kenneth Boa, *Conformed to His Image: Biblical and Practical Approaches to Spiritual Formation* (Grand Rapids, MI: Zondervan, 2001), 404–405.

can confirm through comparing each of these that we have the best text possible without the originals.

Because we can trust the accuracy of the Bible, we can trust its contents. We can verify most of the historical and archaeological matters mentioned in the Bible. So it is accurate to history also. Why are no other Scripture texts like the Hindu Vedas or the Qur'an subject to the same rigorous testing? The only thing that is left is to discover the message of faith and respond to it.

3. **How do you know Jesus actually died on the cross?**

Jesus' death on the cross is a historical fact based on several things. First, his trials would have been a matter of public record. Second, no one can ever know how many thousands of people witnessed this historical event. Third, of those eyewitnesses, three of them wrote Gospels, and the fourth (Luke) extensively interviewed eyewitnesses to the event. These are the ways that historians verify a historical event. We can be certain that Jesus died on the cross.

4. **How can God even have a son?**

The idea of having a son seems peculiar to us. It doesn't make sense that God, a spiritual being, can have a son, a physical being. However, the virgin birth is attested in the Gospels (Matthew and Luke), and prophesied by Isaiah (Isaiah 7:14). Jesus, God's Son, is his son not as a descendent but as one who is like him in substance. The Son of God is expressing the familial relationship between God the Father and Jesus. It is not describing his physical makeup or beginning, because Jesus does not have a beginning. God has a son that is like him in substance but not in person, much like a father has a son who is in substance like him but in person different than him. As far as the virgin birth, the Holy Spirit overshadowed Mary so that Jesus only had a heavenly Father.

5. **How can you be sure there is a God?**

No one can prove that God exists. But the evidence for him is so weighty and numerous that most people believe in God. Humans seem by nature to worship something or someone. No matter where you go in the world, you'll find humans who have some type of religious or belief system. After looking at all of the evidence, chance does not seem to cut it. In Christian teaching, God is a Supreme Being, outside of creation who is the Master of the Universe. Almost every human being throughout history maintained that God exists. The question really is, "Which God is the right one?"

6. Why can't I wait until I die to find out if it's true?

We only have this human existence to accept Christ as our Lord and Savior. At the moment of death or Christ's return, it will be too late to make a decision for him. After we die, when we realize the truth, it will be too late to change a life time of not choosing him. As part of the Pascalian Wager, I would suggest to you that it is better to accept Christ now and find out after death it wasn't true, still being a good person with no loss to your soul. Otherwise, if you don't accept him now, and find out it is true after you die, then your soul is lost. As the Scripture says, "Today is the day of salvation" (2 Corinthians 6:2).

7. What do Christians have that I don't?

Christians have an assurance of their salvation, that when they die they will be with Jesus in heaven guaranteed. It is a heavenly inheritance that only belongs to those who know Jesus. Also, in this life, Christians have a high standard of morality, undeniable joy, peace that passes understanding, and a friend who sticks closer than a brother in times of trial. The Holy Spirit dwells in us from the moment of salvation and God's presence is always with us. We never walk alone. There is also the community of faith, the church. Christians share in a common faith, community, and destiny.

8. How can you believe Jesus was more than just a man like the rest of us?

Too many prophecies happened around Jesus' life. He fulfilled all of the Old Testament prophecies about a Messiah, an Anointed

(Chosen) One of God, who would come and save the human race. From his virgin birth to his ultimate sacrificial death on the cross, he fulfilled every prophecy ever written about the Messiah. During his life, he was led by the Spirit and performed miracles, signs, and wonders that are undeniable. Aside from all of this, his teaching and his words were true to the audiences of the New Testament and ring true to us today.

He demonstrated that he was no ordinary human being. God testified that he was his Son (Matthew 3:17; 17:5; Mark 1:11; Luke 3:22). The term "Son of God" in the Bible refers to the deity of Jesus. Israel's religious leaders testified that Jesus called himself the Son of God (Matthew 27:43). The Roman soldier that witnessed his death claimed he was the Son of God (Matthew 27:54; Mark 15:39). Jesus also declared himself to be the Son of God (John 10:36). He rose from the dead, which no other founder of any religion has even claimed to do.

Questions from Kenneth Boa's book:

9. Why believe in miracles?

We believe in miracles because the Bible shows God doing them. It teaches that nothing is impossible with God (Luke 1:37). Jesus did many miracles of various kinds from commanding nature to healing the human body. If God promised and demonstrated miracles, then He can still do them today because He does not change (James 1:17; Hebrews 13:8). Part of living out your faith is to seek the things God makes available to you.

10. Isn't Christianity just a psychological crutch?

There are many atheists who say that Christianity, and all religion for that matter, is just a crutch to make us feel like someone is looking out for us. But I have found that many Christians are stronger in life because of the support group of the church and the belief that God protects, provides, and blesses them. I would challenge atheists that they have little support system and believe they are on their own in life.

As noble as the independent cowboy sounds, living that lifestyle is a completely different matter. We are built to be interdependent on one another. Religion, and especially Christianity, supports this design in us. When we need help, we can ask for it. When others need help, we can give it. These are all part of what it means to be human. Interdependence is one of the hallmarks of psychology.

11. If God is good, why do evil and suffering exist?

God created a good creation (Genesis 1-2). Everything that is good comes from God (James 1:17). He is not the source of anything evil (1 John 1:5). Evil comes from the evil one (Satan, the devil). It originated when humans used their free will to gain what they thought was independence from God (Genesis 3).

Evil is in the world because of sin, disobedience, and rebellion against God. These have caused God's good world to be cursed and to begin to decay. Evil and suffering in the world result from human free will, the desires within our own flesh, and the influence of evil spiritual beings (Ephesians 2:1-3; James 1:13-15).

12. How can Christ be the only way to God?

Jesus stated that he is the Way, Truth, and Life, and that no one comes to the Father except through him (John 14:6). All religions create an exemption in some form. But the truth about Jesus is that he came to this earth in human form (John 1:14) for the sole purpose of leading us to heaven and his Father.

In a world of relativity, secularism, and pluralism, this biblical truth smacks the face of most people you will witness to. Man-made religions are easy to spot. They tend to rely on pleasing the person, enhancing image, and making people feel good. Christianity challenges human beings to become like God and live in a way that denies their flesh.

The exclusivity of Jesus' claim is a tough pill to swallow. But seeing that Jesus has infinite relationship with the Father, he would know how best to reach him. We have his testimony on this matter. Since no one who has died can come back and tell us if it is true, He is the only source who came from heaven once at incarnation and a second time after his resurrection.

The Bible points to him as the ultimate Priest who gave the ultimate sacrifice for humans to be reconciled with God (Hebrews 9:11, 15; 10:11-14; 1 Peter 3:18).

13. Will God judge those who never have heard about Christ?

This is actually a question usually asked by believers rather than unbelievers. Unbelievers may only ask this contemptuously after hearing that Jesus is the only way to heaven. The standard is that you must know Jesus personally to enter heaven. On that basis, Christians often ask about those who have never heard the name Jesus.

The best answer for this question is that God judges every human being individually. We don't really know how he would deal with someone who has never heard about Jesus. It is presumed that Peter is referring to the saints and ancient peoples when he says that Jesus visited them in prison and shared the gospel with them (1 Peter 3:19-20). But this may have been a one-time offer. Once we die, we will be judged. He has done just that since the beginning of the revelation of his Word. At every time, God has offered a way to fall under his protection in salvation. For the nation of Israel, it was his law and sacrificial system. Now it is Jesus, the ultimate fulfillment of both the law and sacrifices.

14. If Christianity is true, why are there so many hypocrites?

God's standards for holiness are extremely high. As Christians attempt to be obedient to the Holy Spirit and follow his ways, we do stumble from time to time. To the world, this looks like hypocrisy. We are still learning to see everyone through God's eyes and treat them the way He treated us. Christians aren't perfect, and we should be the first ones to admit that.

We must also remember that everyone, despite what religion or lack of religion they may have, exhibits hypocritical behavior. Christians are not the only humans on the planet that are hypocritical. Just about everyone is hypocritical in one way or another at one time or another. Avoiding becoming a Christian will not keep anyone from looking like a hypocrite.

15. Isn't a good moral life enough to get into heaven?

A good moral life is a lofty goal. The question is, by whose standards is it a good moral life. "Good" is a subjective term. What looks like a good moral system to me may not look very good to you.

If morality were the only measure to get into heaven, we would all have a shot. The problem is that to get into heaven, we must follow God's moral system. The Bible clearly states often that no one is righteous before God (Romans 3:10-18, for example).

Since we all have failed in obtaining God's moral standard, we must rely on Jesus' sacrifice to get into heaven. It's not about what we can do on our own through our morals, but about knowing Jesus, the person who vouches for our righteousness before God.

16. Isn't just believing in Christ too easy?

Believing in Jesus is easy. But it is also difficult. We can begin following Jesus in one moment, but not finish our journey of belief in him until the completion of our lifetime. A child can understand the Bible, yet adults like me have studied it for our entire lives.

God has made knowing Jesus the only requirement for salvation. But look at how many people reject him or don't know him. Coming to a belief in Jesus is not an easy process. If it were, seekers worldwide would have no questions about becoming a Christian or knowing Jesus.

While the gate is easy to enter, the path to the gate is hard for many travelers. When you get to the place where you know Jesus and are ready to follow him, you have already traveled the longest desert of your life. Once you get to the oasis, accepting Jesus is the easy part. But that also is only the beginning of a lifelong pursuit of knowing God deeper and deeper.

17. What does it mean to believe?

The Bible uses several metaphors for becoming a believer in Jesus. It has been described as becoming a new creation (2 Corinthians 5:17-18), being born again (John 3:3), and putting on Christ (Galatians 3:27). Water baptism is a beautiful image of what happens when we believe in Jesus (Romans 6:1-15).

To believe in Jesus is to trust in his ultimate sacrifice offered on the cross once for all. It is to place your faith in Jesus as the only Way to heaven. Those who believe in Jesus trust him with their physical and eternal lives. They look to Him as the ultimate example of what it means to know and please God. They believe He died, was buried, and three days later was raised from the dead. They trust in him as the Lord and Savior, the Boss of their lives.

18. Can people be sure of their salvation?

Yes. The Bible tells us that God's Holy Spirit in us testifies that we are God's children (Romans 8:16). There is an inner confirmation that trusting in Jesus yields all of the benefits of salvation (Romans 5:1-5; Ephesians 1:3-14).

Beyond this, as we obey the Holy Spirit, we begin to exhibit the changes that God makes in us to make us holy like him. Along with that internal witness of the Holy Spirit is the external witness of our change in lifestyle and behavior. We trust that Jesus has made the difference in our lives that grants us eternal life.

Chapter 7
Leading Seekers to Christ

Because many Christians have never led someone to Christ, they are unprepared for the final step of sharing their faith. Leading the seeker to Jesus is not as difficult as people make it.

The most important and hardest work has already been done by the Holy Spirit by the time a person is ready to accept Jesus and begin living for him. All we have to do is stress the importance of believing in our hearts and speaking with our mouths that belief (Romans 10:10).

After the seeker is sure that they understand the message of salvation, they believe in their heart that what they have heard is the truth. Only God can see the heart. But out of the abundance of the heart, the mouth speaks (Matthew 12:34).

All that is left after believing in the heart is speaking that belief. This is commonly done in two ways. The first is to pray what we call the "prayer of salvation." There is not one prayer of salvation but whatever the heart wishes to speak.

The prayer of salvation is often patterned or modeled by the person leading the seeker to Christ. This is where Christians who share their faith get tripped up or choked up. They are afraid there is a certain prayer that must be memorized or said exactly right. This is not the case.

Leading a person in the prayer of salvation should not be memorized. It should be genuine and fit the situation of a person's salvation. If you have been with them as they have grown to know Christ, their journey should be part of the prayer.

It should be spontaneous and contain the important parts of what it means to believe in Jesus. It can include parts of confessional statements, such as "I believe you died, was buried, and raised from the dead three days later." It can also include ideas such as, "I want you to be the Lord and Savior of my life. I want you to sit on the throne of my heart."

The prayer of salvation should lead the person to express everything they have learned as they have come to know Jesus. It doesn't have to be long. It should be a short acknowledgment of what has already happened in a person's heart.

Take the pressure off of yourself. Don't memorize things to feed into someone else's mouth. Just guide them in a prayer acknowledging that Jesus is the Lord of their life and that they are a changed person. Mention his sacrifice on the cross for them. Mention that they believe their sins are forgiven. Mention that they want to live for Jesus the rest of their days. All of these are simple and should not be complicated.

The second way is the profession of faith a Christian gives when they are water baptized. In most water baptism celebrations, new believers in Jesus are given the opportunity to add their own personal testimony to their public confession of faith. This is where they can affirm their belief in Jesus and testify to what He has done for them already in the short time they have known him.

Chapter 8
What's Next?

Although this short guide has been all about sharing your faith, this is just the beginning step of a long walk with Jesus. We all spend the rest of our lives growing deeper in relationship, knowledge, love, service, obedience to God.

The best inspiration for any of us to share our faith is the danger of our friends and loved ones going to hell. It's the thought of these loved ones coming to know Jesus and serving him as we do.

Our goal is to see them for the rest of eternity with Jesus and us in heaven. Our motivation shouldn't be to rescue people from hell, although that is part of salvation. It should be to see them as God sees them, as his creatures with his image.

It's an adventure to introduce your loved ones, friends, and complete strangers in your world to the Savior of the universe. May we all be encouraged, convicted, and committed to seeing everyone in our mission field begin their relationship with Jesus.

Appendix
Resources for Further Engagement

Evangelism Styles

Building a Contagious Church (Mark Mittleberg)

General Apologetics

CARM.com

Evidence That Demands a Verdict (Josh McDowell)

Logical (Philosophical) Apologetics

Philosophical Foundations for a Christian Worldview (William Lane Craig)

Reasonable Faith (William Lane Craig)

Conformed to His Image: Biblical and Practical Approaches to Spiritual Formation (Kenneth Boa)

The Big Book of Christian Apologetics: An A-Z Guide (Norman Geisler)

Scientific Apologetics

I Don't Have Enough Faith to Be an Atheist (Frank Turek, Norman Geisler)

The Lie: Evolution (Ken Hamm)

The Face That Demonstrates the Farce of Evolution (Hank Hanegraaff)

The Creation Answer Book (Hank Hanegraaff)

Dear Reader

Thank you for taking the time to read my book. I appreciate your support and hope that it helps you to share your faith. May we all have the courage to step out and be used by the Holy Spirit to nudge our family, friends, and even strangers closer to Jesus.

There's another way you could continue to support me. One or more of these actions will give the book more visibility or connect you to everything I'm doing:

- Please leave a review. If you go to the place you bought the book and leave a review, whether good or bad, this helps the book to be more visible in the marketplaces. This is a quick way to support both me and this book.
- Please sign up for my email list. If you are interested in following me or engaging with me more, you can go to my blog at www.Jonathansrock.com and sign up for my email newsletter. You'll get some free short stories and be emailed anytime I release a blog or news.
- Please like my Facebook author page and share my books and posts. Type "Author Jonathan Srock" in the Facebook search box. You'll get even more news about my activities. Also, you can share this book and other resources by me in your social media feeds.

You can always contact me through my blog at www.Jonathansrock.com or my email address (srockenator@Gmail.com). I hope to hear from you!

Blessing,

Rev. Jonathan Srock

About the Author

Rev. Jonathan Srock is an ordained minister with the Assemblies of God for 10 years. He received two Bachelor's degrees in Biblical Languages and Pastoral Ministries, as well as a Masters of Divinity from Assemblies of God Theological Seminary. He was privileged to be the Lead Pastor of New Life Assembly in Shillington, PA for four years before suffering sudden paralysis. Jonathan has been a Christian for about 30 years.

His passion is to help imprint the character of Christ through teaching and preaching God's Word. Rev. Jonathan is part of the PennDel Ministry Network. He is a quadriplegic and lives in Central PA with his parents. He enjoys preaching in local churches, writing books, blogging, and answering questions about God and the Bible. He also enjoys reading, watching sports, and geeking out over computers in his "spare" time.

Made in United States
Orlando, FL
13 March 2024